21 Ways to Increase ... Employee Engagement

Pat Heydlauff

21 Ways to Increase ... Employee Engagement
Copyright © 2017, Pat Heydlauff, All Rights Reserved

ISBN: 978-0-9983347-1-4
Published by: Energy Design
2017

Dedication

To my father, Dave Pastor, who led by example.

Contents

Acknowledgments

I am eternally grateful to my immigrant father. He was a man of few words, but he taught me that truth, honesty, determination, and hard work are the foundation for success. He may have had only a third-grade education, but he led by example. I thank him for instilling in me an "I can do anything I set my mind to" attitude, and that the "university of life" experiences provide the ultimate education—that real learning begins after formal schooling ends.

It is my father's philosophy that allows me to step out of constraining boxes of conformity and into the world of possibilities.

Thank you, also, to my editor, Dawn Josephson, and my graphic designer, Janet Aiossa, for helping to make this book a reality.

Finally, I would like to acknowledge the impact others had on my life:

Walt Disney
Albert Einstein
Steve Jobs
The Cheshire Cat, Alice in Wonderland
Yoda, Star Wars

Thank you all for your inspiration and many life lessons.

A Note from the Author

I wrote this book for the millions of hard working decision-makers, thought-leaders, and employees who realize that a stable economy and traditional methods of communication and operations came crashing down around organizations and institutions with the advent of the new millennium. This up-heaval continues to exponentially increase causing chaos and disengagement in the workplace.

But I didn't write just a series of books; rather, I want to take you on a transformational journey, including the process of change and the new tools needed to meet the demands of a radically changed 21st century workplace. This is an empower-ing process that will provide you the roadmap and tools to overcome the complexities of a multi-generation, disengaged workforce, while increasing performance and productivity at all levels.

Leaders, whether corporate or entrepreneurial, and employees have been working with 17th century operating systems and tools that urgently need to be upgraded to the 21st century and beyond.

If you think of yourself as you are today, you will remain as you are tomorrow. But if you think of yourself as you want to be, you will become what you envision. Likewise, if you think of your company as it is today, it will remain as it is tomorrow. But if you think of your company as you want it to be, it will become what you create.

This book sets up for you the habit of proactively being responsible for yourself, empowering yourself to create your future, and then empowering your employees to create a unified future for the organization and themselves. Because old systems no longer work, the only way to change your influence on a problem and others is to change your habits and methods for the way you influence others. This series will provide you the tools to do just that.

> If you think of yourself as you are today, you will remain as you are tomorrow. But if you think of yourself as you want to be, you will become what you envision.

I'm giving you an empowering philosophy with practical application, not a bandage or quick fix, but a process with practical tools to shift your thinking and results so you can increase productivity on a business and personal level.

This book is your facilitator of transformation to help you create a better tomorrow where employees are engaged, encouraged, and involved. This system has an action plan with measurable, tangible results that positively impact bottom line profits, improving efficiency as in time and things, and improving effectiveness as in dealing with people.

If you thought you were efficient before, now you are going to see how outdated some of the traditional thinking is and how far superior this system is to anything you've done before. You are going to learn how to maximize your time, conserve your personal energy, and obtain superior results within your organization. You will see a difference in your day, improvement in your communications, and have everyone on the same page.

This is going to upgrade everything *you've been doing*, and *you* will be able to upgrade your workforce. By the time you've read this series of books, you will be capable of all of the above.

Introduction

Hone
Your
Focus

*You, your peers, your workforce, and associates are always focusing on something all of the time, but is it what **you** want them to be doing?*

Focus (or attention) is much like the wind. If harnessed and channeled, the wind can create electricity, expedite the flight of an airplane or the movement of a ship, and pump water from a well. You cannot stop the wind nor change its intensity or at times destructive forces, but when harnessed, the wind is useful and productive, generating a limitless supply of focused energy.

Just as you can't stop the wind, you cannot stop focus or where your team's attention is flowing. You, your peers, your workforce, and associates are always focusing on something all of the time, but is it what **you** want them to be doing? The key is getting yourself and others to focus on the right things and to avoid the distractions. The good news is that you can harness and channel focus so it is engaged in what you want and generates the productivity and performance you desire.

Where is YOUR Focus?
In the movie *Gone with the Wind*, the last line of the prologue introducing the epic novel simply reads: "A civilization gone with the wind." Is this what is happening every day with your personal focus and that of your workforce?

15

Focused thought tied together with action is the critical link when it comes to the forward movement of performance and productivity. If, like in the movie, your flow of focus is gone with the wind, you need to take steps now to harness and channel your attention, because that is what yields productivity, performance, and profitability. When gone with the wind, focus responds to constant interruptions, distraction, and self-destruction.

Two great examples of people who not only had great clarity of vision but also unwavering focus are Steve Jobs and Walt Disney. If you think about it, both were great innovators. Both were engaged in creating a product that their customers didn't know they needed or wanted, and both employed laser focus on their ever-expanding vision. Without the laser focus, their visions could not have become such enormous success realities.

> Focused thought tied together with action is the critical link when it comes to the forward movement of performance and productivity.

Disney didn't want to produce just another cartoon or build another merry-go-round or amusement park. His vision was to create an ultimate end-destination entertainment experience for children of all ages, from toddler to senior, to create the happiest place on earth. And Jobs didn't want to produce just another computer. He wanted more than the bite of an apple; he wanted to create communications links, systems, and equipment that could be invisible assistants anticipating your every need while keeping you connected to everything, everywhere, and everyone.

Jobs and Disney were innovators par excellence and their legacy speaks highly of their infinite creative genius and focus. Their focus wasn't distracted with minutia, imperfection, and partial solutions, but rather honed and sharpened with laser accuracy. It was their intense focus that engaged their work-force, allowing them to rise to the top with innovative product offerings through productivity, performance, and profitability.

Understanding the Flow of Focus

Focus flows to and from many directions and is either engaged in productivity or distracted by unbridled chaos. Being aware of how focus flows in your workplace and personal life is the first step to harnessing and channeling it to increase produc-tivity and performance.

Only when you realize how many ways focus can be distracted can you begin to develop a roadmap to the harnessing process so you can unleash it at your choosing and send it in the direc-tion you want.

Once accomplished, you will be in possession of the same leadership secret weapon that Steve Jobs and Walt Disney unleashed and used so effectively. In this eBook, I will reveal some of the steps for har-nessing and unleashing that flow of focus as it relates to your physi-cal workspace. We will discuss ways to optimize your surround-ings so focus can reign and chaos can diminish. We will also cover strategies to relieve mental and digital distractions that lead to loss of focus.

> Being aware of how focus flows in your workplace and per-sonal life is the first step to harnessing and channeling it to increase productivity and performance.

Ultimately, I will share tools to help you become more aware of where the flow of focus goes and help you develop a roadmap to harnessing and unleashing it so you can improve your own success as well as those you lead.

Chapter 1

Ignite
Laser
Focused
Engagement

It's not about getting people more engaged, nor is it about tapping into their engagement.

Rather, it's all about focusing the engagement they already have.

Make no mistake: Public enemy number one for leadership and management is distracted focus. It leads to lack of clarity and reduces personal and workforce engagement, productivity, and performance. Change the focus dynamic in your life and you will improve your personal performance, engage your team, and improve long-term success.

Unclear goals and distracted focus slow your productivity and limit profitability. You can eliminate distracted focus and harness it to maximize productivity by first acknowledging that there is a natural flow to focus in your life and in the workplace.

Observe the number of distractions that interrupt the flow of your focus and what happens to it and the focus of your team in just one 24-hour period. You will quickly realize that focus needs to be protected and harnessed so it can be unleashed on productivity and performance, not the most recent crises or minutiae. Watch for some of the following distractors and interruptions:

- Telephone/cell phone calls and text messages, business and personal
- Social media and email intrusion
- Peer pressure
- Associates stopping by to chat
- Want-to-be emergencies
- Disenfranchised team members sabotaging productivity
- Lack of clarity in goals and objectives
- Poor communication of goals and objectives
- Complex instruction

Once you've observed the impaired attention and concentration, the distraction of irrelevant stimuli, the frequent shifts from one uncompleted task to another, and see what is occurring right in front of you, you will be ready to make some simple changes necessary in your workplace and mindset to unleash the power of focus.

Why Distracted Focus is so Dangerous

Research shows that at any given time, only 30 percent of the workforce are engaged and inspired at work. Roughly 20 percent of the employees are actively disengaged. The other 50 percent of American workers are present but not necessarily engaged or inspired by their work or their managers.

Actually, upon reflection, the 50 percent that are present are engaged in something, but is it what you want them to be engaged in? Not likely. It doesn't take a genius to determine that 70 percent of most employees are disengaged. The cost of disengagement is high:

- Higher absenteeism
- Increased workplace accidents
- Reduced productivity
- Lowered profitability

This list can only grow exponentially depending upon the complexity of your organization and the size of your workforce.

Re-Defining the Workplace Environment

So, how do you focus your workforce's engagement? That's the magic question, isn't it?

First, realize that it's not about getting people more engaged, nor is it about tapping into their engagement. Rather, **it's all about focusing the engagement they already have**. This begins in the workplace environment.

Are you letting focus slip away, sending it away, and/or letting it go of free will somewhere else? Worse, have you unknowingly created a workplace environment that contributes to the rapid disbursement of focus or allows it to get stuck in the minutia of the mundane and mediocre? Do you have distractions built into your workplace that break their flow of focus?

> People already know they need to focus, but they don't understand that there is a flow to it. Unfortunately, distracted focus is everywhere in most office environments.

People already know they need to focus, but they don't understand that there is a flow to it. You need to understand what interrupts the flow of focus in your workplace environment and what you can do to create an environment that helps your team focus on meeting the organization's needs and requirements.

Unfortunately, distracted focus is everywhere in most office environments. Physical workplace environment distractions are common such as clutter, improper positioning of management away from their staff, poor arrangement of desks and office furnishings, colors on wall that encourage dysfunction or anxiety, and no clear visuals to nurture focused engagement.

When you add the complexities created by electronic communications like texting, tweeting, and a need for constantly being in contact but not connected, it all adds up to a constant drain of focus. It sets up roadblocks to the flow of your workplace focus, allowing the focus of your engaged workforce to meander to the next urgent issue, whether relevant to the designated objective or not. In the remaining chapters we will discuss ways to eliminate or minimize physical roadblocks to focus and develop guidelines for distracting electronic disruptions and interactions.

> When the flow of focus in your workforce is not harnessed and channeled to meet your needs, production and profitability suffer while employee stress and anxiety increase.

With today's high-tech, low-touch instant gratification world, harnessing the flow of focus of your workforce is critical. There is a natural flow to the focus of your workplace just like there is a natural flow to a production line or the movement of a river. When a river goes out of control like the mighty Mississippi, it can upend people's lives, wreak millions of dollars of havoc, and destroy everything in its path.

Similarly, when the flow of focus in your workforce is not harnessed and channeled to meet your needs, production and profitability suffer while employee stress and anxiety increase. That's why you need to develop a roadmap that harnesses and channels focused engagement by creating a workplace environment where focus is nurtured—where the physical workplace is conducive to focus and mental and digital distractions are minimized. By doing so, your workforce will be both engaged and focused on the task at hand and understand its role within the long-term company vision.

Start with the End in Mind
If you're ready to reclaim the focus of your team, it's critical to start with the end in mind. Starting with the end in mind, or what I call rear-view mirror thinking, is an extremely effective leadership strategy. You can employ this strategy very successfully when you already have an engaged focused workforce. For our purposes right now, this strategy will help you create that engaged, focused workforce.

First, some clarification: Rear-view mirror thinking is not about rehashing the strategies of the past. Unfortunately, leadership and management often use rear-view mirror thinking to look from the present backward to see what used to work and try to improve upon it, or worse, simply repeat it. Industrial Age and Information Age leadership principles do not apply to doing business in the 21st century. History no longer plays a significant role as a direct roadmap to the future. Sure, it gives perspective and guidance, but it no longer ushers in the future.

> Rear-view mirror thinking means to start with a vision of the future you want to create and then outline the steps you need to get there.

When I talk about rear-view mirror thinking, I mean starting with a vision of the future you want to create and then outlining the steps you need to get there.

While there are many things you can learn from Industrial Age masters such as Thomas Edison or Henry Ford, the greatest amount of knowledge needed today is from the future, not the past. Rear-view mirror thinking is about visioneering the future and taking the steps to make that reality happen today.

Of course, for each leader, the end-result of visioneering and creating the future may be different, but their goal is always the same: To achieve an engaged, focused workforce that operates at peak performance. Following are two key questions that will help guide you in this process:

- **Is your workplace prepared for productivity?**
  Is your workplace conducive to the flow of your focus for your workforce and in alignment with the end-result you wish to achieve? Or is your workplace, including offices and cubicles, chaotic and filled with energy drainers and focus distractors? Are there stacks of papers to be filed, piles of magazines unread, boxes of old papers waiting to be sorted and disposed of along with too many things crammed into space that is too small? All of these are focus draining distractors.

  Workplace surroundings help you and your team focus so you can work cohesively and productively and ultimately function at peak performance. When the workplace is disorganized and filled with focus drainers, distracted focus will reign, reducing the productivity and efficiency of the entire team and handicapping everyone's performance. The result of a distracted-focus team is drained physical and mental energy, increased stress and frustration, and reduced productivity.

  Maximum productivity and performance require that the workplace always be organized, paperwork filed, stacks of stuff put away, and that which is no longer relevant discarded. Make sure a minimum of 80% of the workplace is always visible and free of focus-distracting clutter for maximum productivity and peak perfor-mance, including the tops of desks and cubicles.

- **Do you have a focus strategy?**
  If you do not create a focus strategy or a roadmap with your group, their focus will become distracted focus and they will be consumed by their co-workers, associates, peers, social media, cell phone, and family interrup-tions. There will be no flow of focus left for productivity and performance. Peak productivity does not happen without an enforced strategy.

  Later we will create a focus strategy to eliminate dis-tracted focus. I encourage you to enforce it just as you would a mandatory health assessment or dress code. Distracted focus happens and productivity drops every time a member of your team is involved with a text, a tweet, or a personal phone call.

  Make distraction-free focused time the number one pri-ority if you want to improve productivity and efficiency while reducing stress. Well-meaning co-workers, social media, and unintentional interruptions caused by to-day's high-tech low-touch world of electronics by default create distracted focus even in a totally engaged work-force.

When you prepare your workplace and workforce with a clear uninterrupted flow of focus, your fully engaged and focused workforce will create the future you clearly laid out in your rear-view mirror or "end in mind" roadmap.

As a reminder, to successfully use the rear-view mirror thinking, always begin with the future and work back to the present. Then create a roadmap to get you where you want to go. The following chapters will help you with your desired roadmap.

Key Points

1. Change the focus dynamic in your life and you will improve your personal performance, engage your team, and improve long-term success. *What can you do today to improve your focus?*

_____

_____

_____

_____

_____

_____

_____

_____

_____

_____

_____

_____

_____

2. Research shows that at any given time, only 30 percent of the workforce are engaged and inspired at work. The other 50 to 70 percent are either completely disengaged or merely present at work. *What percentage of **your** workforce is currently disengaged? What is disengagement costing you?*

_____

_____

_____

_____

_____

_____

_____

_____

_____

_____

_____

_____

3. The goal is not to get people more engaged, nor is it about tapping into their engagement. Rather, it's all about focusing the engagement they already have. *What signs of engagement have you witnessed in your employees? How can you focus that existing engagement?*

_____

_____

_____

_____

_____

_____

_____

_____

_____

_____

_____

_____

_____

4. You need to develop a roadmap that ignites, harnesses, and channels laser focused engagement by creating a workplace environment where focus is nurtured—where the physical workplace is conducive to focus and mental and digital distractions are minimized. *What distractions do you see in your office or workplace?*

_____

_____

_____

_____

_____

_____

_____

_____

_____

_____

_____

5. Engage in rear-view mirror thinking. This is about visioneering the future and taking the steps to make that reality happen today. *What is your future vision? What steps will get you there?*

_____

_____

_____

_____

_____

_____

_____

_____

_____

_____

_____

_____

_____

Chapter 2

Room Dynamics Fuel Focus and Success

Any change in your workplace always starts with YOU!

So if you want your workplace to change, you have to take the first step and change yourself and your personal area.

W hy is it that some days your productive flow really works and you're in the zone ... and other days you're not? It's all about the way the flow happens. Often, your environment can enhance what you are doing or it can produce obstacles. In fact, the workplace environment changes the productivity and the people in it. For example, let's take a look at a very successful attorney.

Although it was a beautiful, sunny spring day outside, there was a dark cloud hanging over attorney George ... and his office reflected it. George was the managing partner of a multiple-city statewide law firm.

He complained about how unfocused, distracted, and disorganized he felt. He was worried that the firm wasn't going to grow and make money on his watch.

George was also concerned that he was not as efficient and productive as he should be, which left him feeling ineffective as the firm leader. He knew one of the keys to building the firm and increasing business had to do with relationships— they needed to improve relationships to expand existing business and create new relationships to get new business. He complained, "It's as if things are standing in my way, preventing me from accomplishing my goals and challenging my abilities."

Energy Drainers are Everywhere

A cursory glance around George's office easily shed light on the things standing in his way. Displayed on the lengthy window sill of his corner office were at least two dozen framed photographs of family members, kids, fishing buddies with the "big" catch, clients, and more. That's a lot of eyes watching him perform and events distracting him. But that was just the beginning.

- Stacks of files were on the desk, credenza, and floor.
- His CPU was placed under the corner of the L-shaped desk so he would bump into it every time he moved from his computer screen to another area of his desk where he would write and take notes.
- He had poor hearing in his left ear but his phone was still placed on that side. Every time he answered it (with his right hand) he had to reach across his body and the computer screen and keyboard.
- A bookshelf was filled with books he hadn't used in years that could easily reside in the firm's library.
- Several pieces of art gifted from key clients leaned up against a wall because he was unsure of where to hang them.

Each was a significant energy drainer and disrupted his focus. It was no wonder he felt unproductive, couldn't focus, and was always distracted. Either he couldn't find it, it wasn't arranged for efficiency, or it was distracting so his flow of focus was always broken.

Harness Focus to Ignite Productivity

Fortunately George's office had one thing going for it: the placement of his desk and chair. It was on the far side of the room facing the door, which is the most powerful and effective location. Therefore, when sitting in his chair, no matter which area of his desk he was working from, he always had a complete view of the door, and was always aware of people coming and going. His subconscious mind was never distracted nor operating in the flight or fight mode.

With his desk and chair already placed for maximum leadership power, focus, and productivity, it was easier to bring the remainder of his office into alignment with his objectives using these corrections:

- All but three of the personal pictures on the windowsill were eliminated, leaving one with his family, one with his best friends, and one with a major client. This removed a lot of the distractions and channeled the flow of his focus to what was really important in his life.
- Energy-drainers, clutter, and files were either organized in upright files on his desk for current cases or on the credenza for longer term cases. Other items were filed, tossed if possible, or moved to the firm's archives. This lack of organization consumed a lot of his time—time he could have spent cultivating new clients or nurturing existing clients.
- Misplaced equipment like the CPU and his phone were relocated to improve efficiency and increase productivity.
- The bookshelf was totally removed from his office and replaced with a small table and chairs for a more casual meeting area with clients and improved client rapport. We also added a live plant, which provided living energy in the room.
- The pictures were appropriately hung throughout the office; the ones behind the desk of his largest client's wetlands artwork placed emphasis on existing clients.

The artist rendering of George arguing a case in front of the Federal Court was placed on the wall facing him to remind him of past successes and encourage future wins.

The Result

Here is the new layout of George's office:

Attorney's Office Layout

This is a corner office with windows on the south and the west. The office door leads out to attorney's assistant, the office manager and two floors of the firm.

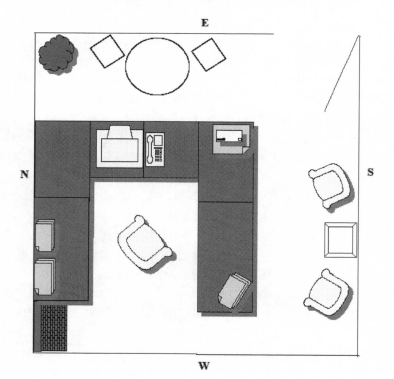

Changing the room dynamics provided George an environment where he became more focused and improved his concentration. He found he had more time to connect with not only the other partners in the firm, but also existing and new clients, making him more efficient and effective.

At the firm's annual retreat four months later, George was recognized for outstanding achievement and honored by the other partners because of his leadership and the fact that he personally brought in more business in those four months than the entire previous year.

> Chaos, clutter, and distractions will immediately disengage your workforce and break their focus, resulting in reduced productivity and diminished performance.

As you can see from George's example, workplace environments matter. Chaos, clutter, and distractions will immediately disengage your workforce and break their focus, resulting in reduced productivity and diminished performance. This type of workplace environment also increases the stress and workload of management, making them scramble to figure out what went wrong, why, and how to fix it.

By applying some key workplace organization principles to your office, you, too, can dramatically improve your flow of focus, fueling efficiency, effectiveness, and productivity. Let's discuss this in more detail to show you how.

It's Time to Improve Your Flow of Focus
Now is the time to adopt the spring cleaning principle. Spring cleaning is a phrase that is usually relegated to the home, but it is just as relevant to the well-being, productivity, and future of a small business or a large corporation.

Spring cleaning is the practice of cleaning a home from top to bottom, especially after long, hard winters in colder climates. This process not only removes stagnant energy from a closed-up house in the winter and eliminates any leftover germs, but also removes clutter, making way for new energy and prosperity to enter. In the workplace, spring cleaning can be any kind of heavy duty office cleaning, painting, organizing, or getting business affairs in order.

Start with Your Personal Workspace

Any change in your workplace always starts with YOU! So if you want your workplace to change, you have to take the first step and change yourself and your personal area. When you clean up, get rid of clutter, and organize your personal workspace, you eliminate chaos and disorganization and replace it with effectiveness and improved performance.

So let's begin. Take a look at your workspace right now. (No tidying up before starting this exercise!)

- Is your workspace clean? Or is there dust on your surfaces, last week's take-out lunch containers littering your bookshelf, or an overflowing trash can?
- Is your workspace efficiently laid out and clutter free? Or are there stacks of files to get to, magazines to read?
- Is your desk clear of distractions? Or is only 20 percent of your desk visible?
- Is the floor clear of clutter, boxes, and files? Or can you barely enter your workspace?
- Are your walls mostly empty with well-appointed pictures that are uplifting or encouraging? Or are the walls constipated by being covered with distracting pictures, posters, and post-its?
- Is your email inbox manageable? Or is it overflowing with unread messages?

How did you do? Were you able to answer "yes" to the first question of each bullet? Or did your answers lean toward the second question of each bullet? If you're like most people, the second set of questions gained more "yes" answers. But don't worry! You can change all that starting now. Here are some suggestions to get you started.

- When sitting at your desk are you facing the door? Or is your back to the door (or an opening as in a cubicle)? If you cannot position yourself so your back is not to an opening or a door, place a small mirror on your desk so you can always see someone approaching from behind. This will increase your focus and reduce anxiety by preventing unexpected distractions.
- When you enter your workspace or sit at your desk, whether in the corner office or a cubicle, you need to see 80 percent of it clean and clutter free so you can work at peak performance.
- The same rule of thumb applies to your desk. You cannot be effective if you are constantly distracted by paperwork, pictures, and mounds of clutter piled high on your desk, on tables, or in boxes on the floor.
- This rule also applies to personal pictures and belongings that manage to collect on your walls, window sills, and the top of your desk. Severely limit personal pictures. Your mind wanders to each pictured family member or friend, wondering what they are doing or if they are okay. They distract your focus every time you look at them, which reduces your productivity and performance.
- The cleaning and de-cluttering process also applies to your computer. Here are some specific strategies for dealing with your computer clutter:

o Your desktop screen should have 80 percent or more of the screen surface empty so you don't begin the day feeling overwhelmed, distracted, and behind.

o Set aside time weekly to manage, delete, and organize electronic information.

o Organize your desktop so everything is easily accessible. You might put all of your social media links on the right side and your working programs and folders on the left. Eliminate the duplicates. Try using the great colorful folders that are available as a download to organize important programs or projects. For example, you could use green folders for new clients, new business, and growth; the red folders for established clients that provide you continued business; and the yellow folders for less important but still necessary information.

o Your screensaver or desktop background choice can either provide you positive supportive energy, or it can add to the clutter by giving you negative or stressful energy. The more neutral and calm the background, the more productive, efficient, and effective you will be.

o Organize and/or eliminate the folders inside your computer. Do you save everything you create into folders in your My Documents folder, or are they just stashed somewhere but you are not really sure where or how to access them at a moment's notice? The old adage "time is money" really applies here. If you can't find something you need, you become less efficient and productive, perhaps losing a customer, a sale, or the last chapter of a book you thought you finished two months ago. Organizing makes information more accessible and you more efficient and eliminating the clutter makes your computer more efficient.

o Stop being a slave to your email inbox. Make a decision right now that nothing is more important than being in-control of your time and productivity. Turn off the sound on your email inbox so it isn't a distraction and doesn't scream at you with urgency. Remove yourself from all email lists and newsletters that aren't necessary for your job. Notify everyone that you will be checking your inbox only twice daily, late in the morning and late afternoon and will respond promptly. Moreover, be sure to handle email information only once. Read it and take action, then file it or delete it. This will increase your productivity and limit unimportant email interruptions.

- Discard anything not used regularly and organize the rest for efficient use. Do you have outdated procedure manuals sitting on your bookshelf? Are your file cabinets full of papers that are six years old and totally irrelevant to your work today? If so, get rid of them.
- Make impersonal open space, such as cubicles and work stations, more inviting and personal by adding a plant or a mini fish tank. If you also wish to have a bit more privacy, create a mini wall of plants or use a larger fish tank.

Here are two images that show optimal layouts for an office and a cubicle:

Office Layout

Optimal Placement of Desk and Chair
Office door faces east, the direction of good health, new growth and new business. The desk is organized to promote maximum productivity.

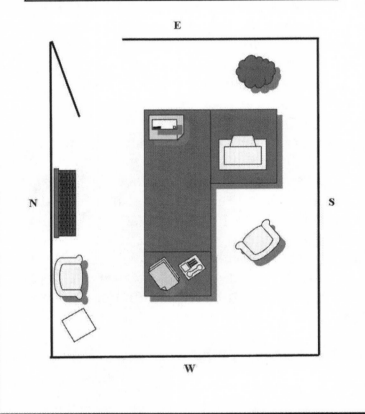

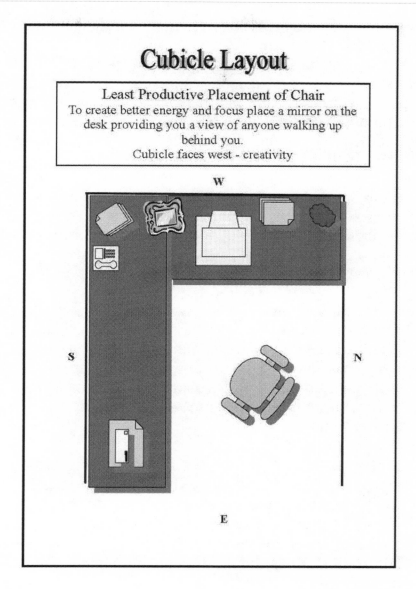

By taking these steps in your personal workspace environment, you will experience a boost in performance and will be able to face the larger task of engaging the workforce to do the same in the shared workplace environment.

Eliminate Chaos and Distractions
in the Entire Workplace Too

Help employees set up a workplace environment to that enables them to be more focused, especially on what you want them to focus upon so they can perform better. The flow of the environment determines how the people feel when working in their specific environment. The better they feel, the more productive they will be.

The reason for spring cleaning the business workplace environment is simple. When you clean and improve their workplace environment, you engage the workforce, improve their productivity, and maintain their loyalty and their retention, which improves employee buy-in and your profitability.

Leave your office, cubicle, or workspace and look around your entire facility. Look at the physical environment your employees work in eight hours or more per day. What do you see? Is there a natural flow of focus and productivity that moves through the layout, or are there obstructions? The little known secret is that focus is flowing somewhere, like a river, but is it flowing where you want?

- Is the physical layout of the office space or production area set up to maximize efficiency, productivity, and safety, inviting employees to want to be there? Or is it inefficient, depressing, and unwelcoming?
- Is the office well-lit with natural light or full spectrum light bulbs? Or is the lighting too harsh with fluorescent lights?
- Are the walls painted calming productive colors? Or are they dirty and in disrepair?
- Are office or production supplies located near their appropriate work areas? Or are they a long walk away, using up precious time and money to access them?

- Is noise pollution under control? Or is it so loud that it's difficult to concentrate?
- Is the atmosphere encouraging, engaging, and conducive to maximum performance? Or is there a constant feeling of chaos?
- Are the hallways easy to access? Or are there boxes of new retail inventory or spare manufacturing parts strewn along hallways so employees can barely walk through?
- Is everything put away in its proper place? Or do you see old equipment and stacks of paperwork that you should have disposed of long ago?
- Is management located within their team area? Or are they floors above or in another building, making them inaccessible?

How did you do this time? Were you able to answer "yes" to the first question of each bullet? Or did your answers lean toward the second question of each bullet? If you're like most people, the second set of questions gained more "yes" answers. But don't worry! You can change all that too!

In this case you'll need to engage the workforce's participation first by showing them the benefits of the spring cleaning process. Since actions speak louder than words, you can assure them that they will feel better while on the job and tasks will be easier for them to do because everything is organized—because you have already done it and experienced the results. Additionally, let them know they will reduce their stress and anxiety levels because they will be able to find everything they need at a moment's notice; and because everything is in its place, they will be more productive, which in turn makes the business more profitable and potentially ensures the company's sustainability and their jobs.

While the shared office space can be a much larger project than your personal workspace, you would attack it the same way.

- Evaluate the physical layout of your organization and the way employees and offices are placed for maximum efficiency and employee engagement. Make changes as necessary to improve the flow of focus and productivity.
- Discard and de-clutter to eliminate chaos. Clutter is a barrier to focus, engagement, and productivity. Clutter causes disorder and confusion resulting in distraction, misperception, and misunderstandings. Clutter acts like a tree planted in the middle of a road, confusing the driver and creating a roadblock. Therefore, address clutter right away. File it, store it, organize it, or get rid of it. Hallways and walkways are not storage areas where stacks of boxes should be stored. Everyone will be more efficient.
- Scrub floors, shampoo carpeting, and paint walls a calm color. Cleanliness makes everyone feel better about being there eight hours or more per day.
- Use specific colors on the walls that reduce stress. For example, light green or blue are very calming yet enhance the flow of productivity, especially in the area of sales, accounting, and IT. Light earth tone colors like salmon, peach, or flesh tones are great for customer service and operations. Stress and anxiety levels will go down and performance will increase.
- Check all equipment to make sure it is placed properly. Also ensure that everything is working, and fix anything that needs to be repaired or replaced. The workforce will be more efficient.
- Make sure workstations and regularly used supplies are in close proximity, so less time is lost and efficiency increases.

- Ill placed walls are huge barriers to the flow of focus. No one really likes to work in a 6' x 6' or 2'x 4' box, especially Generations X and Y. Perhaps it is time to eliminate the cubicle or to re-create it to better facilitate the flow of focus and engagement of your workforce.

- Place equipment and locate people for efficiency, to save time, and to have immediate access. For example, place the department head within the team, not in an inaccessible ivory tower office. Employee engagement and productivity will increase.

- Pay specific attention to the way the flow of focus moves throughout your organization. For example, if two departments work closely together don't separate them by miles of walls, cubicles, and red tape. Both departments will be more effective and innovative.

- Take time to actually view your workplace environment from the perspective of your team to see if it is conducive to engagement and focus. If not, it's time to change.

- Share the 80 percent rule and encourage employees to maintain their workspace and desktop a "clutter free zone." Provide "clutter free" prizes to encourage this process. Engagement will improve.

- ***Together*** make a list of all of the other things that can be done in the workplace to make it a more pleasant place to work. Employees will feel valued.

- Don't limit this process to just spring. Put it on the calendar to review every four to six months and repeat as needed but at minimum, annually.

As you go through this process, remember to always lead by example. If you can do spring cleaning in your workspace and maintain it, they can do the same and your organization will benefit from increased productivity and profitability.

It's important to step out of the existing top down management thinking box so you can actually see what your workforce faces on a daily basis. Make changes to the physical environment so you can connect with your workforce emotionally. Create a workplace environment that is calm, encouraging, and engaging—where focus flows freely. The result? Productivity, profitability, and performance not only grow but are also sustainable.

Key Points

6. Your workplace environment's room dynamics matter. Chaos, clutter, and distractions will immediately disengage your workforce and break their focus, resulting in reduced productivity and diminished performance. *After analyzing your workplace, how are chaos, clutter, and distractions affecting you and your employees?*

_____

_____

_____

_____

_____

_____

_____

_____

_____

_____

_____

7. Take an honest assessment of your personal workspace and your entire office environment. Assess such things as clutter, efficiency, noise levels, wall color, and furniture placement. *What can you do differently in your physical environment to maximize your personal focus?*

_____

_____

_____

_____

_____

_____

_____

_____

_____

_____

_____

_____

8. Any change in your workplace always starts with YOU! So if you want your workplace to change, you have to take the first step by cleaning up, getting rid of clutter, and organizing your personal workspace. *What one thing can you do **today** to take the first step in the change process?*

_____

_____

_____

_____

_____

_____

_____

_____

_____

_____

_____

9. When you clean and improve the entire workplace environment you engage the workforce, improve their productivity, and maintain their loyalty and their retention, which improves your profitability. *What is your plan for getting everyone on board and involved in the cleanup process?*

_____

_____

_____

_____

_____

_____

_____

_____

_____

_____

_____

_____

10. Ultimately, clutter is a barrier to focus, engagement, and productivity. Clutter causes disorder and confusion resulting in distraction, misperception, and misunderstandings. Clutter acts like a tree planted in the middle of a road, confusing the driver and creating a roadblock. Remove the clutter today. *Make an action list of everything that must be removed or rearranged ASAP.*

_____

_____

_____

_____

_____

_____

_____

_____

_____

_____

_____

Chapter 3

Mental Strategies to Hone Your Focus

When both your workspace and your mind are clutter-free, you'll be able to find what you need at a moment's notice.

You'll get things done faster, you'll respond to requests in a timely manner, and you'll automatically be more productive.

Now that you understand what room dynamics has to do with productivity and why clearing physical clutter is so important, it's time to talk about clearing the mental clutter so you can increase your efficiency.

Just as creating a strategic workplace environment will maximize your productivity, efficiency, and effectiveness, creating a mental plan will improve your performance. When both your workspace and your mind are clutter-free, you'll be able to find what you need at a moment's notice, you'll get things done faster, you'll respond to requests in a timely manner, and you'll automatically be more productive.

Why Mental Focus is So Important
Research shows that a three second distraction (or loss of mental focus) doubles errors, and a four-and-a-half second interruption triples errors. Are numerous daily distractions wreaking havoc on your productivity and efficiency?

When was the last time you placed a "do not disturb" sign on your door? If the answer is "never," today is a good day to start. Research by both Michigan State University and the U.S.

Navy has determined that errors are made immediately after interruptions, even if the interruption lasts only a few seconds.

Whether you are working on a massive long-term project or a brief e-mail to an associate, distractions cause a loss in focus that can be both costly and time-consuming. Focus is the single most important tool in your arsenal for being efficient, effective, and productive.

- A great vision without focus can never be achieved.
- A great team that is not focused cannot achieve the vision.
- And a great idea when not focused upon will become irrelevant, stagnant, and worthless.

Remember, Walt Disney dreamed about creating the greatest magical destinations in the world and succeeded due to his devotion to his vision, determination, and focus. Steve Jobs created electronic tools that consumers never dreamed of because of his vision and intense focus. Both of these innovators were successful because of their ability to eliminate mental clutter and focus on their unique visions.

Create a Focus Plan that Improves Performance
Distractions, interruptions, and multi-tasking are often forced activities in a busy work schedule. It is important to first recognize that such interruptions can dramatically lessen your productivity and impair efficiency. Once you realize how much damage they do, it is time to create a plan to remove the distractions and maintain your focus. Here are some guidelines to help.

- **Shut Your Door**
  Improving your performance comes through focus. And focus comes from a quiet space where concentration can be maximized. The only way to achieve quiet space is to

shut the door and keep out the interruptions and distractions. You can even place a "Do Not Disturb" sign on your door to warn peers and associates that you are focused on a specific project or issue. If you work in a cubicle or open workspace and don't have a door, use some other visual cue to let others know you can't be interrupted. For example, you can tape a huge "do not disturb" sign on the edge of the cubicle, put a similar tent sign on your desk, or even be daring and use yellow crime scene tape until others get the message. Be sure to include on the sign the time they can return to speak with you.

Remember, every time you are interrupted you have to shift gears mentally, causing a major break in your focus. When you maintain your focus, you improve your performance while increasing your efficiency and productivity.

- **Schedule Interruption Time**
  Set aside specific time for multi-tasking and interruptions. Depending upon your circumstances it can be the last 10 minutes of each hour. Or you can schedule half-hour time segments twice in the morning and twice in the afternoon to deal with necessary but non-urgent issues. The only time you should be interrupted as needed is for an urgent matter (see next point for what "urgent" means).

Let others know that during these scheduled time windows, they will get 100 percent of your undivided attention. They will soon recognize that 100 percent of your undivided attention is much better than your divided attention while you are still trying to process what you were concentrating on when they interrupted you. By actually scheduling such time, colleagues will be less likely to interrupt you and you'll all be more productive.

When doing this part of the plan, you will have to determine exactly what works for your type of workplace and business. However, a working strategic plan that everyone is aware of will minimize your downtime while increasing everyone's productivity and efficiency.

- **Know What's Urgent**
  Focus on the important, not the urgent. Urgent matters will come up and require you to divert from your scheduled interruption time. That's just part of business. But only you know what is important and what can wait. Therefore, make it clear what items or situations are so urgent that they should be allowed to step in front of something else.

  When an "urgent" matter comes up, the only way to make an intelligent decision about whether you should divert your attention from what you are working on is to evaluate the two items side by side. Then you can assess if the urgent item is truly urgent or if it is someone else simply bringing you their problem to solve.

- **Eliminate Energy Drainers from Your Daily Schedule**
  Determine what is preventing you from completing the important things on time. Are there time-devouring items on your calendar you can eliminate? Do social media and electronic communications take a huge bite of time out of your schedule? Are all of those necessary interruptions nibbling away at your time, or can you delegate a specific amount of time before lunch and before the end of the day to check those communications?

If there is specific information you need, set up a special sound code for your VIP messages so you can retrieve them immediately, yet leave the less important for later. It's your time that you are losing and your efficiency that is suffering. *Eliminate what you can and control what remains.*

- **Create a High-Five Priorities List**
This list should be created before you even set foot in your workspace on Monday and should contain only the highest priority items. Routine daily tasks should not go on this list.

Start with your most important items; the more important the item, the higher it is placed on the list. When you are ready to tackle these, ALWAYS begin with item number one. If it is a long-term project, still begin with it first then move on to the next item(s) on your list. This will dramatically improve your focus and productivity.

- **Turn Off All Electronic Equipment**
For maximum focus and concentration, eliminate the constant flow of electronic distractions. This list includes your cell phone, the e-mail received sound on your computer announcing that you have mail, all social media, and any other devices that may interrupt you. There are untold hours of productivity lost and errors made due to the interruptions of electronic equipment and social media.

Personal tweets, Facebook time, posting on Instagram, and connecting with family members are the greatest distractors of all! Social media should be relegated to off hours. Family interruptions, unless an emergency, should be limited. Therefore, make sure your family knows your schedule and is onboard with your time windows.

Harness the Power of Silence

For you, silence is golden. Silence, yes, *silence,* is a powerful mental strategy and leadership tool. You've likely heard many adages about silence, such as "he who speaks first loses" or "silence is golden," which comes from a longer phrase "speech is silver, silence is golden," placing a much greater value on silence, not just the spoken word.

From the workforce engagement perspective, silence is not golden. Research by New York University's Stern School of Business Department of Management and Organizational Behavior shows that the workforce is remaining silent. This type of silence is not a good thing, though. In fact, it is something to avoid or overcome at all cost. Silence on the part of the workforce means you have no upward communication about organizational problems or issues concerning the workforce.

On the other hand, silence on the part of the leader and management offers an opportunity for the workforce to express themselves more openly, and in fact encourages such action as long as the communication is received non-judgmentally. Silence is all about social, cultural, internal, and relational interaction. Silence is often the missing link when it comes to verbal and non-verbal communications. And it's key for harnessing your mental focus.

> Silence is a powerful mental strategy and leadership tool. It is a powerful use of personal energy and a great way to hone your mental focus.

Silence is a powerful use of personal energy and a great way to hone your mental focus. The list below will help you use silence to switch off distractions, increase your leadership skills, and become a stronger leader.

- **Use Silence to Gain Clarity**
  "Silence is the sleep that nourishes wisdom," said Francis Bacon, English philosopher and statesman. If you have an endless loop of chatter congesting your thinking, in addition to external distractions and interruptions, it is very difficult to remain focused on the task at hand or achieve clarity to innovate or resolve issues. Once your surroundings and mind become silent, you will turn your thoughts inward and achieve the clarity you seek. Set aside at least five minutes per day to spend in absolute silence. The clarity will come and the innovation will flow. This will improve effectiveness and employee engagement.

- **Use Silence to Stay in Control**
  "Silence is one of the hardest arguments to refute," stated Josh Billings, pen name for humorist Henry Wheeler. When you are in a difficult situation that demands your focus, such as a negotiation or confrontation, silence is your best friend. In such situations your silence empowers you and removes a sense of control from others. If this is difficult for you to do, mentally count to 10, 20, or even 30 before speaking. That provides you time to think and stay in control.

- **Use Silence to Focus Your Communication**
  "To communicate through silence is a link between the thoughts of man," said Marcel Marceau, French actor and mime. Silence is the perfect way to say to someone, "You are important. I am listening to you." Silence al-

lows you time to not only listen, but also give importance to what you are hearing. It helps remove the emotions from an issue and provides calm in the midst of a storm. The strategic use of silence allows the workforce to speak up without retribution. They feel heard, not judged. They will voluntarily seek you out to communicate their needs and point out problems. Practice remaining silent so you can hear.

- **Use Silence to Encourage Ideas to Flow**
  "Nothing strengthens authority so much as silence," stated Leonardo da Vinci, a leading figure of the Italian Renaissance. Not only did da Vinci believe that silence strengthened authority, but also vastly expanded one's ability to think and focus. Spending much of his time in silence creating and doodling, da Vinci wound up inventing, painting, sculpting, studying science, and conceiving an endless stream of innovative inventions, often the precursors to our modern day weaponry. It was the silence that allowed the ideas to flow into his consciousness. It was the silence and observation that provided the fertile ground that allowed him to create masterpieces like the *Mona Lisa* or *The Last Supper* on blank canvases or the blueprint for a modern day helicopter. At least once a week put aside time to be in total solitude and empty your mind of the distractions. Physically turn off electronic equipment, put your cell phone on airplane mode, and find the peace and creativity of absolute silence. Keep a pen and paper nearby to record your thoughts after you return from your mental silent retreat.

- **Use Silence to Emphasize a Point**
  "Well-timed silence hath more eloquence than speech," was the advice of Martin Farquhar Tupper, English writer and poet. When you are the one speaking, be very

aware of the use of silence when making a point. Silence adds value and significance. Your silence makes the listener take note of what you just said and think, "I'd better remember that." The listener will wonder why what you said was so important and they will look forward to your next statement. Silence is the non-verbal exclamation point at the end of a sentence or bold formatting, telling everyone to **pay attention**. This takes a bit of practice but is very effective.

Choose to incorporate silence into your day and you'll quickly find that silence is the secret weapon that fuels your personal flow of focus, self-control, and innovation. Remember that everything you say or don't say plays a role in your mental focus. The key is to use this power wisely.

Mental focus was one of the keys to the enormous success of Walt Disney and Steve Jobs. Finding a way to stay focused and stop shifting gears is critical to your success and the success of your company. Therefore, develop your own strategy using the suggestions provided, and begin today. By incorporating your own mental focus plan into your daily routine, you will maximize the use of your precious time, thus improving your focus and increasing your efficiency.

Key Points

11. When both your workspace and your mind are clutter-free, you'll be able to find what you need at a moment's notice, you'll get things done faster, you'll respond to requests in a timely manner, and you'll automatically be more productive. *What steps can you take to reduce daily mental distractions for you and your team?*

---

12. Research shows that a three second distraction (or loss of mental focus) doubles errors and a four-and-a-half second interruption triples errors. *Are numerous daily distractions wreaking havoc on your productivity and efficiency? Which specific distractions are the most troublesome for you? How can you eliminate or at least reduce them?*

_____

_____

_____

_____

_____

_____

_____

_____

_____

_____

_____

_____

13. You need a mental focusing plan to improve your performance. *What are the top three action items for your mental focusing plan?*

_____

_____

_____

_____

_____

_____

_____

_____

_____

_____

_____

_____

_____

14. Silence is a powerful mental strategy and leadership tool. *How can you incorporate more silent time in your day?*

_____

_____

_____

_____

_____

_____

_____

_____

_____

_____

_____

_____

_____

15. Silence helps you gain clarity, stay in control, focus your communications, encourage ideas, and emphasize a point. *Which of these benefits is most important to you? Why? What steps will you take today to harness some of the benefits?*

_____

_____

_____

_____

_____

_____

_____

_____

_____

_____

_____

_____

Chapter 4

Social Technologies Fuel the Flow of Focus

Social technologies provide the never-before available speed and scale of the Internet, zero marginal cost, lowered barriers, and interaction with large or small groups across all geographies and time zones.

U nlike the 1980s and 1990s, the speed of change today is transformative. The cause of this warp speed change: social technologies, according to a July 2012 study, "The Social Economy: Unlocking values and productivity through social technologies," by the McKinsey Global Institute.

The study states that there are greater than 1.5 billion networking users globally and 80 percent of them regularly interact through social networks. Yet only 70 percent of businesses use social technologies, most on a limited basis. Of those, 90 percent acknowledge some benefit, but only three percent feel they derive a substantial benefit from social technologies.

There is no doubt that social technologies such as social media, online purchasing, networking, publishing, email, mobile apps, research, and simply connecting online have caused sweeping cultural, economic, and social change. People get married online, technology can cause governments to fall, and people can purchase anything from a golf ball to a house ... all thanks to the digital revolution.

The Technology Flow of Focus Opportunity

Social media technologies are all about collaboration and content creation rather than just consumption. The opportunity lies in the fact that social technologies are fast becoming an important business tool because of the exponential flow of information. This can either be good for the flow of focus or it can create huge distractions. It all depends on your mindset.

The study states that social technologies have enormous potential to:

- Raise productivity of knowledge workers
- Extend the capabilities of high-skill workers
- Streamline communication and collaboration
- Lower barriers within the organization
- Import additional knowledge and expertise from extended networks

All of this can lead to an increase of $900 billion – $1-3 trillion of annual value!

The adoption of social technologies on the business level will be driven by the need for innovation, advances in technology, economics, and speed. Social technologies provide the never-before available speed and scale of the Internet, zero marginal cost, lowered barriers, and interaction with large or small groups across all geographies and time zones.

Most people automatically think external communications or connections when considering social media applications to business. But the real value to the business community is internal. Social technology platforms should be applied within to the flow of communications, knowledge sharing, and collaboration. According to McKinsey, when social media technology is fully implemented, the productivity of interactive workers, high-skill knowledge workers, managers, and professionals will increase 20 to 25 percent. The improvement in productivity of these three categories has a domino effect and raises the productivity of the overall business. This is an incredible increase in the flow of focus ... if that is where you want your employees to focus.

One might think budget, time, talent, or desire might be the obstacle(s) standing in the way of creating a 20-25 percent rise in productivity. No, it is the business' corporate culture. In order to capitalize on such great opportunity, major organizational transformation must also take place. A corporate environment must be created that is filled with trust, respect, and equality when it comes to thoughts and ideas—a workplace where the physical, emotional, and mental environment is conducive to unleashing the flow of focus and innovation. This new environment demands that a strong vision is in place, requires a nurturing environment that spawns innovation, and engages the workforce and customer through the use of soft skills.

> You must create a corporate environment that is filled with trust, respect, and equality when it comes to thoughts and ideas.

Digital Helpers or Digital Addiction?
Of course, with any discussion of employee engagement and technology, the issue of distraction comes up. Everyone understands the benefits of being in a digital age, but is there a down side?

Dementia usually describes deterioration in cognitive abilities that are commonly seen in people who have suffered a head injury or psychiatric illness. Digital Dementia, a term coined in South Korea, is used to describe a deterioration of cognitive abilities resulting from over-use of computers, smart phones, gaming consoles, and the Internet in general.

Dr. Byun Gi-won of the Balance Brain Centre in Seoul, Korea said, "Over-use of smart phones and game devices hampers the balanced development of the brain ... heavy users are likely to develop the left side of their brains, leaving the right side untapped or underdeveloped." It is the right side of the brain that is linked with concentration, creativity, innovation, and emotional development. Digital Dementia includes other side effects such as problems with attention, organization, orientation, problem solving, social communications, and reasoning—a huge problem when trying to engage employees.

> If your employees show problems with attention, organization, orientation, problem-solving, social communications, and reasoning, it may be a sign that Digital Dementia is in your workplace.

With Digital Dementia on the rise, does the overuse of digital gadgets and electronic media foreshadow eminent decline of business innovation? Do using social technologies have more risk than reward? And what impact does it have on the engagement and flow of focus of your employees?

Today's technological society has been raising and embracing two generations of employees or potential employees that are so digitally focused with brains not fully developed that they can no longer remember even the simplest of things, such as a phone number. This will have great impact on the business community in the areas of productivity, efficiency, communications, social interaction, and employee/employer connection. Additional research shows that more than 60 percent of employees studied, between the ages of 20 and 30, suffer from memory loss and forgetfulness, blaming an environment overwhelmed by digital devices. With employees who have impaired concentration and memory spans, how do employers cope with people who lack innovative, critical, or creative thinking?

Dealing with a Digital Tsunami

Even if you are not currently dealing with the Digital Dementia problem, you will be—and soon. You will find it creeping into and lowering your productivity and performance levels, causing communication and harmony issues and resulting in multi-generational workforces being further segregated, thereby setting up connection and blame-game failures. Here are two key suggestions for making social technologies and technology in general work for you so you can reap its rewards.

- **Recognize the Digital Tsunami Before it Arrives**
  By being forewarned you can be prepared. It will save you hundreds of work hours trying to figure out how to correct the avalanche of problems after they've happened and are entrenched in your workforce. Create a checklist of behavioral issues symptomatic of Digital Dementia that are already problematic and getting worse. Recognizing that there are social and memory-based issues caused by the advancement of technology is the first step in dealing with it.

- **Go on the Offense**
  Create a plan to either prevent or deal with the deficiencies of Digital Dementia so it doesn't cripple the productivity and profitability of your business. Consider the following:

- o Build a team to deal with this impending digital tsunami. Include a person from every level of your organization.
- o Make them aware of the current research and the long-term effects of Digital Dementia on your organization and their personal lives. This tsunami will flood into every crevice of your organization and the devastation will move quickly like wildfire.
- o Create a plan that involves all employees interacting on an in-person level—not just digital face time.
- o Limit the use of digital devices in the workplace when and where possible.
- o Change the environment by painting walls colors more conducive to interpersonal relations, such as a pastel terra cotta (light salmon or flesh tone) or a light green with a touch of blue.
- o Meet with employees at their work stations instead of emailing or texting them. Even a telephone call is better than a text or email.
- o Require that everyone memorizes certain things like your company vision or safety rules to help build up concentration and boost memory.
- o Hold regular innovation and creativity meetings as a group to engage everyone in the process of developing the right side of the brain to compensate for the digitally over-controlled left side.

This list just scratches the surface of some of the steps you can take today to overcome the Digital Dementia that is facing your business. Remember, your workforce is always engaged and focused on something. It is important that they are focused on what your business needs to thrive and grow, not just digital technology that usurps their time and attention.

Don't Let Speed Derail Your Focus

In addition to the addiction problem, social technologies challenge your focus because of the speed at which information is available. You've probably noticed that communications are becoming exponentially more complex and instantaneous with each passing day. There is zero time delay between continents as information, good and bad, swiftly passes through the electronic communications universe and social media. It is the speed of the information that is also a problem, as the speed can derail your focus.

> Without honing your ability to create and interpret messages lightening fast, you will quickly lose focus and your productivity will diminish.

Now more than ever, you must make split second decisions about the information you receive, namely whether the information is true, deliberately deceptive, or simply an uninformed opinion. Without honing your ability to create and interpret messages lightening fast, you will quickly lose focus and your productivity will diminish.

Numerous researchers, scientists, and futurists predict that technology will advance exponentially in the next 20 years. But at what cost? Compassionate human interaction and understanding, social skills, kindness, and the ability to get along with others in a meaningful way have already suffered significantly.

Gone are the days of employee interaction face-to-face. It is much easier to send an abrupt retort or express a non-helpful negative comment via an emotionless non-empathetic text or email. It happens all the time on social media. But when it happens in the workplace, focus, productivity, and engagement take a nosedive.

The truth is, when you are constantly distracted by tweets, texts, emails, and posts, it is almost impossible to maintain quality productivity. Each of those interruptions not only disrupts what you are doing but is delivered with emotions and feelings that do not serve you well in the workplace.

Steps to Consider for Disconnecting and Improving Productivity

If you feel you might need a digital intervention in order to regain your focus, here are some suggestions.

- Evaluate the amount of time you spend online connecting with impersonal others. How does that compare with the amount of connecting with family, friends, and business colleagues in real life? No one can tell you what is right for you; but until you know the answer to this question and compare it to all the other things available for you to do in life; you will not realize the impact of being online.

- Record the number of workplace interruptions that occur daily or hourly from being online. Pay specific attention to how much time is devoured by these distractions and how long it takes you to get your focus back on track so you can be more productive.

- Evaluate whether being online interferes with personal downtime. How much time do you spend connecting that could be better used for self-motivation, self-inspiration, or uplifting your spirit? Balance is illusive and impossible to achieve without quiet time to reflect and regenerate.

If you feel that digital distraction has taken over your world, confiscated your time, and reduced both engagement and productivity, determine what works best for you and take action. Go cold turkey and put technology away for one day over the weekend so you can really get reconnected with your personal life. If that is frightening, start with disconnecting one hour per day. Doing so will make a huge positive difference in your life, your relationships, and your productivity.

Social media technologies have dramatically increased the speed of everything, be it good, bad, or neutral. Change no longer cranks along at a snail's pace but rather moves on a millisecond scale over the Internet. And this definitely impacts your focus.

While there are many opportunities for growth and profit thanks to technology, there are challenges and risks involved too. Make a solid plan for dealing with the digital revolution so you can reap its rewards, enhance your productivity, and maintain your focus.

Key Points

16. Social technologies have enormous potential to raise the productivity of knowledge workers, extend the capabilities of high-skill workers, streamline communication and collaboration, lower barriers within the organization, and import additional knowledge and expertise from extended networks. All of this can lead to an increase of $900 billion – $1-3 trillion of annual value! *How can you better use social technologies to reap these rewards?*

_____

_____

_____

_____

_____

_____

_____

_____

_____

_____

17. Digital Dementia, a term coined in South Korea, is used to describe a deterioration of cognitive abilities resulting from over-use of computers, smart phones, gaming consoles, and the Internet in general. Research shows that more than 60 percent of employees studied, between the ages of 20 and 30, suffer from memory loss and forgetfulness, blaming an environment overwhelmed by digital devices. *What signs of Digital Dementia do you see in your workforce? How is this impacting your bottom line?*

_____

_____

_____

_____

_____

_____

_____

_____

_____

_____

_____

18. You need a plan to either prevent or deal with the deficiencies of Digital Dementia so it doesn't cripple the productivity and profitability of your business. *What are the top three action items you can implement to deal with Digital Dementia in your workplace?*

_____

_____

_____

_____

_____

_____

_____

_____

_____

_____

_____

_____

19. Today's speed of information is a problem, as the speed can derail your focus and disengage your workforce. Now more than ever, you must make split second decisions about the information you receive, namely whether the information is true, deliberately deceptive, or simply an uninformed opinion. *How can you help your employees make the needed quick decision without wrecking their focus? What additional training or support can you provide?*

_____

_____

_____

_____

_____

_____

_____

_____

_____

_____

_____

20. If you feel that digital distraction has taken over your world, confiscated your time, and reduced both engagement and productivity, determine what works best for you and take action. *What would happen if you put technology away for one day over the weekend so you can really get reconnected with your personal life? When will you give this a try? Schedule it now!*

Conclusion

Fuel Focus to Move Beyond Engagement

What are you focusing on?
What is your workforce focusing on?

Everyone is always focusing on something.
Is it the right thing?

How you use your time and what you focus on determines the quality of your performance and effectiveness. What are you focusing on? What is your workforce focusing on? Everyone is always focusing on something. Is it the right thing?

As you can see from all we've discussed, fueling focus is perhaps your most important workforce engagement strategy. Energy, time, and money are expended whether you and your team are focused on the results you want or not. Is your workforce using their mental, emotional, and spiritual energy to improve productivity and increase sustainability?

There's no doubt that the workplace environment impacts the productivity and the people in it. You can either engineer your environment to be more productive and focused (and see productivity soar), or you can leave things as they are (and keep everyone and everything stagnant). The choice is yours.

Focus is like water. It flows where it flows and either you harness it and take advantage of the flow or you don't. Everyone's days are filled with distractions. That's simply the nature of business. So it's all about how to keep employees focused

93

when there are so many things pulling them in different directions.

I'll leave you now with three key points about the importance of focus:

- **Focus mental energy** – Use clearly stated goals, including time frames, for your workforce. When work is prioritized, it is easier to keep distractions to a minimum. Your workforce must know exactly what it should be doing in order to achieve the results you desire. Not only explain their objectives, but also give them measurable time and quality parameters they must meet. Explain your expectations *visually*, *verbally*, and *emotionally*. **Then have them play back their understanding of what your expectations are.** Only then will you be sure they have a complete focused mental understanding of their responsibilities.

- **Focus emotional energy** – Create a distraction-free workplace environment that is uncluttered, organized, and conducive to productivity. Things like *lighting, colors of the walls, noise pollution, and visual appearances* have an emotional impact on employees. The more comfortable and happy they are in the workplace, the more productive they will be. Employees spend almost half of their waking hours in the workplace environment. When you create an environment that is more welcoming, they become more focused and productive. They also are more engaged and focused on the outcome, which can range from improved productivity to increased profitability.

- **Focus spiritual energy** – Create a recognition and regeneration program. A broken spirit does not perform at the top of his or her game. This is a two-step process.

1) Start by saying "thank you" often. Explain the role the workforce plays in the future sustainability of the company, and acknowledge the contribution made by all employees. Engage your team in creating a recognition program so they can better appreciate the reward—perhaps providing an ice cream day with management serving the team or a team outing to the amusement park or movies. **Make the acknowledgement public if you want to make a huge difference.**

2) Offer ways for everyone to nurture their inner spirit by providing a quiet room for meditation, reading, or even yoga. Create a mini library filled with all types of inspirational books, quotes, and short videos to be used at breaks or lunchtime. Fill and update bulletin boards (these are not passé) regularly with inspiring quotes and stories. Do the same electronically via internal Facebook pages and email messages. They will be more engaged and focused on what you ask of them.

The result of incorporating everything in this eBook into your workplace environment is improved employee retention, enhanced morale, a more efficient workspace, and increased productivity—all of which leads to increased profitability and sustainability. Begin today. Your successful future depends on it.

Key Point

21. Now that you've completed this eBook, *what is your complete action plan for increasing employee engagement and improving everyone's flow of focus? When will you implement your plan?*

_____

_____

_____

_____

_____

_____

_____

_____

_____

_____

_____

_____

About the Author

Pat Heydlauff has spent the last 25 years designing groundbreaking strategies and developing tools crucial for navigating through the diverse workforce of today.

She is acutely aware of the contributing factors that impact productivity and the bottom line. The age of the workforce has changed and so has social communications. Distractions, disengagement, and disrupted focus exist, which Pat addresses in her unique, groundbreaking Flow of Focus System.

With the ultimate goal to build corporate sustainability, Pat's Flow of Focus System achieves:

- Increased Productivity
- Improved Efficiency
- Boosted Profitability

Pat increased the bottom line revenue by 300% in less than 5 years as the CEO of the Nutritional Food Industry's national trade association by creating a strategic road map that increased productivity, innovation, and sustainability. With her belief in her groundbreaking Flow of Focus System—including room dynamics of the workplace, communication, connection, and control of time—Pat helped turn the Nutritional Food Industry Association around to a thriving organization. Her customized flow of focus system serves to inspire leadership, Board interaction, and employee performance.

Pat is a Palm Beach County, Florida resident and is active in the Florida Speakers Association. She works with small to medium corporations, organizations, and non-profits using her 7 Step "Flow of Focus" System that provides a roadmap for leadership, executives, management, and the workforce to manage their personal focus, efficiency, and effectiveness while improving all aspects of the business. She shares her innovative tools through consultation, programs, and publications, providing industry leaders easy-to-apply strategies to create a roadmap for improved productivity, sustainability, and increased profitability.

Speaking Topics & Training Programs

Pat offers the following business and leadership programs. Select from her high content presentations for decision makers and influence leaders seeking a strategic advantage and a groundbreaking "flow of focus" approach to leadership. All presentations can be customized for your specific needs of topic and length of program.

Engagement 3.0: Creating the Focused and Profitable Workforce

Create a workforce environment where employees are focused, encouraged, inspired, empowered and appreciated so they voluntarily buy-in raising their productivity, improving their performance, reducing stress and look forward to coming to work. The Orbital Look at a corporation – spatial, verbal, mental and emotional.

- Learn how to use the flow of focus in the physical environment as a strategic advantage
- Develop a flow of communications – get off the soapbox to engage
- Create a flow of connection – implant the vision of CEO into the heart of the worker
- Develop a flow of time – do the important vs. the urgent
- Implement employee recognition and appreciate – result is buy-in
- Instill a flow of regeneration for leadership so they can be innovative and pass that onto employees while controlling stress
- Implement sustainability by eliminating resistance to change

6 Essentials to Eliminate Distractions & Fuel Employee Productivity

The workforce environment either enhances the employees' focus and productivity or is an obstacle. Changing the dynamics of your workforce environment by eliminating distractions and chaos leads to a more efficient, effective and productive employee.

- Create workforce environments for maximum engagement, focus and productivity
- Eliminate energy-drainers that distract
- Organize for efficiency
- Apply organization and distraction principles to electronics and equipment
- Use color and design to change the workplace experience and improve the outcome
- Shift the flow of focus to improve engagement, self-motivation, enthusiasm, productivity and ROI

The Big Picture: How to Focus Distracted Agendas

Given the diversity in age and social communication and connection of the employee population consistent communication is getting harder. Develop an orbital flow of communications and interpersonal connections for leadership and the workforce so know that the message is being heard as intended while creating workforce buy-in. Not only does this lead to profitability but create focused engagement which leads to innovation.

- Eliminate soapbox communications – create an orbital flow to get feedback
- Create audible, kinesthetic, visual ways of communicating

- Create an internal Social Network to improve communications and relations
- Have Management connect face to face with the workforce or create regular C Suite internal messaging – provide for a private flow of messaging back
- Locate management strategically within the workforce
- Develop strategies to help the workforce understand why they are doing what they are doing and how it is connected to the outcome
- Improve connection and engagement – value employees – acknowledge and appreciate them – they matter and want to know it
- Create a corporate vision that ignites your workforce

Laser Focus: 7 Strategies to Manage Interruptions and Maximize Productivity

When you are in control of the flow of your time, it brings you balance so you can better discern how to prioritize your time. You will be more efficient and effective which yields peak performance.

- Create "focus time" and "focus space"
- Manage your calendar don't let it manage you
- Control/Limit distractions and interruptions – both physical and electronic
- Learn the benefits doing the important versus urgent
- Create interruption appointment windows and collaboration time – everyone will be more engaged
- Create time balance – learn to Evaluate what to delegate or streamline so you can be more focused, maximize productivity, and reduce stress
- Make room for self-motivation

Innovate: 6 Ways to Avoid Corporate Burn-Out and Create a Fired-Up Team

Regenerate leadership so innovation flows through the workforce—leadership can't change the workforce environment and productivity if they don't change themselves first. Energy follows focus and thinking. Engaged leaders lead by example.

- Regenerate to provide a flow of creativity to solve problems and innovate
- Regenerate to create a calmer workforce - lowers stress levels
- Regenerate to refuel – it's not enough just to workout / physical activity
- Regenerate to eliminate emotional and mental burnout
- Regenerate to connect with creativity and innovation – it takes more than knowledge and sport
- Regenerate employees with in-house mini creativity sessions for employees to lesson stress, improve engagement and ROI

Palm Beach Gardens, FL 33418

Phone: 561-408-2708 ~ Fax: 561-408-2710

www.engagetolead.com   info@engagetolead.com